WITHDRAWN FROM

Sir John S. D. Thompson

The pushover who died too soon

Written by Elle Andra-Warner

Illustrated by Suzanne Mogensen

Photo Credits
JackFruit Press Ltd. would like to thank Library and
Archives Canada for images appearing on pages 1, 9,
11, and 52. Thanks also to the Supreme Court of
Canada (photographer Philippe Landreville) for the
photograph of the chief justice that appears on page
19; P. Widling for the image on page 31; and the
Buckinghamshire County Council for the image on
page 37.

© 2007 JackFruit Press Ltd.
Publisher — Jacqueline Brown
Editor - Joerg Ostermann
Designer and Art Director — Marcel Lafleur
Researchers — Barbara Baillargeon and Hagit Hadaya

Thank you to Judge Marvin Morten of Ontario for his
assistance with the "Hot Topic" box on judges (p. 19).

All rights reserved. No part of this book may be
reproduced, stored in a retrieval system, or transmitted,
in any form or by any means, without the prior written
permission of JackFruit Press Ltd. or, in the case of
photocopying or other reprographic copying, a licence
from The Canadian Copyright Licensing Agency (Access
Copyright).

For an Access Copyright licence, visit
www.accesscopyright.ca or call (toll-free)
1-800-893-5777.

JackFruit Press Ltd.
Toronto, Canada
www.jackfruitpress.com

Library and Archives Canada Cataloguing in Publication

Andra-Warner, Elle,
Sir John S. D. Thompson: The pushover who died too
soon / written by Elle Andra-Warner; illustrated by
Suzanne Mogensen.

(Canadian prime ministers: warts and all)
Includes index.

ISBN 978-0-9736406-8-7

1. Thompson, John S. D. (John Sparrow David), Sir,
1844–1894—Juvenile literature. 2. Prime ministers—
Canada—Biography—Juvenile literature. 3. Prime
ministers—Nova Scotia—Biography—Juvenile literature.
4. Canada—Politics and government—1867–1896—
Juvenile literature. 5. Nova Scotia—Politics and
government—1867–1896—Juvenile literature. I.
Mogensen, Suzanne II. Title. III. Series.

FC526.T4W37 2006   j971.05'5092
C2006-903429-X

Printed and bound in India

... So, I'm here to show you around this really cool series of books on great Canadians.

This book tells the story of Sir John S. D. Thompson, Canada's fourth prime minister.

He died only two years after becoming PM. In spite of this, he left his mark on Canada in a lot of important ways.

Contents

Hot topics

Sir John S. D. Thompson:

Our forgotten prime minister

He exchanged coded love letters with his wife. He died at the royal dining table. And he might have been one of Canada's greatest prime ministers. But Sir John Sparrow David Thompson shocked the nation by dying at age 50, barely two years after he became Canada's fourth prime minister and just hours after he received a great honour from **Queen Victoria**.

He had just sat down in the royal dining room with the queen at **Windsor Castle** in England, when he collapsed and died on December 12, 1894. After lying in state at Windsor Castle (the only Canadian prime minister ever to do so), his body was placed on a black-painted British warship that took him across the stormy waters of the Atlantic Ocean back to his hometown, Halifax, for burial.

"I'm glad that I found him"

Although he died young, John left a lasting legacy on the fledgling new country of Canada. He negotiated important fishing treaties between Canada and the United States, even as the countries were capturing each other's fishing boats. He was an outstanding lawyer and a co-founder of Nova Scotia's famous **Dalhousie Law School**. He also drafted and developed the Canadian **Criminal Code**. He campaigned for equal rights for men and women, aggressively advocating for women to have a vote, but he died before he could make any changes to Canada's laws. It would be another 24 years after his death before women could vote in Canada. He knew that in the future Canada would be a bilingual country and encouraged his own children to be fluent in both English and French.

Want to know more? The words in bold are explained in the glossary at the back of the book.

John had already had a successful career as a lawyer and as a provincial politician when, in 1885, at age 41, he became the **attorney general** of Canada. Prime Minister **Sir John A. Macdonald** liked John and told a colleague, "I'm glad that I found him." When the **Conservative** government was looking for a successor to the aging Macdonald, John was considered the best candidate to take over as prime minister.

But there was one nasty problem: the powerful Ontario Conservatives considered him a pervert. Don't jump to conclusions—the word "pervert" had a different meaning than it does today. Back then, pervert was the term for a Protestant who had converted to **Roman Catholicism**. John, born a **Methodist**, had converted to Catholicism when he was in his mid-20s. The Ontario political power-brokers said they could accept a born Catholic, but not a pervert.

This is why, when Macdonald died in 1891, it was 70-year-old senator **Sir John Abbott** who reluctantly became Canada's new prime minister. Abbott hated both politics and his new job. Everyone knew, however, it was really John who was running the government. When Abbott resigned the following year, the time was right for John to be the next prime minister—and this time the Ontario politicians agreed. On December 5, 1892, 48-year-old John David Thompson was sworn in as Canada's first Roman Catholic prime minister.

Behind every great pervert . . .

No introduction to John would be complete without mentioning the most important part of his personal and political life—his beloved wife, Annie. She was the driving force in his life, directing his political career to the top spot in Canadian politics. Their courtship and devoted marriage is one of the great Canadian love stories. When they were apart, John and Annie wrote each other long, passionate love letters, sometimes two or three a day, using shorthand as a lover's code so no one else could read their words.

It was Annie (and Sir John A.) who pushed John to stay in politics, even though he repeatedly told them he wanted out. His dream job was Supreme Court judge, in Halifax, where he could work and stay close to his family. But Annie and Sir John A. would remind him that Canada needed him and that there would be time in the future for him to have his way.

When John died on December 12, 1894, he'd spent almost half of his life in politics. Today, few Canadians have even heard of him. He has become Canada's forgotten prime minister.

You can thank John for your Labour Day holiday. Without him, you'd be back to school after the summer break a few days earlier!

Prime Minister Macdonald likes Thompson and tells a colleague, "I'm glad that I found him." When the Conservatives start looking for a successor to the aging Sir John A., Thompson is considered the best candidate.

There's just one nasty problem. The powerful Ontario Conservatives consider John a "pervert" and will have nothing to do with him. Fortunately, they'll change their minds about this.

1827

John's father leaves Ireland to try his luck in London, England. It doesn't work out, so he sails across the Atlantic Ocean to find success in North America. Promising his family he'll return in four years, he books passage to Nova Scotia.

He arrives in Halifax in May 1827. At that time, Halifax has a population of around 16,000. It's a crowded place where downtown streets are planked and the houses are built tightly together on small lots with tiny backyards. And there's a stench in the air. Most of the houses have outhouses because there's no sewage system in Halifax. Can you imagine the smell coming from the backyards on a hot summer day?

8

Chapter 1

From dropout to top lawyer

Sir John Sparrow David Thompson's roots go back to Ireland and Scotland. His father, John Sr., left the family home in Waterford, Ireland in the spring of 1827 and sailed across the Atlantic Ocean to try his luck in North America. He arrived several weeks later in Halifax, Nova Scotia.

Halifax in 1827 was a town of 16,000 that had grown quickly from a British naval and army base. It was a crowded place where the downtown houses were built tightly together on tiny lots with small backyards . . . and there was a stench in the air. Most of the houses had outdoor toilets (they called them privies) because there was no sewage system in Halifax. Can you imagine the horrible smell coming from the backyards on hot summer days?

A wonderful new life

John Sr. had planned to move on to the United States, but a year later was still in Halifax. He sent glowing letters to his family back home in Ireland, telling them about his wonderful new life. To his older brother William he wrote that "Halifax is a pretty place" and told about sipping tea with **Joseph Howe**, the 24-year-old editor of the

1844
John is born.

1847
His 15-year-old sister dies of dropsy.

1848
His 18-year-old sister dies of dropsy.

1854
Here he is, aged 10.

1860
He begins to study law by working for a lawyer.

1865
John becomes a full-fledged lawyer and starts his law practice.

1867
He supplements his income by working as a shorthand reporter for the Nova Scotia Legislative Assembly.

In the summer, John's older brother, Joe, dies of yellow fever.

His father dies in October.

He meets his future wife, Annie Affleck.

Nova Scotia becomes part of the Dominion of Canada.

John's father had many different jobs. One of them included being a shorthand reporter of government speeches. He taught John how to write using this special, cryptic code.

John used shorthand in his legal work and to write love letters to his wife. It was a different code from the one in use today.

Consider this: the fastest you can write by hand is 35 words per minute (wpm), yet people speak at 150–180 wpm. The world record for shorthand, on the other hand, is 350 wpm for two minutes!

Halifax newspaper, the *Nova Scotian*. They become lifetime friends. Howe would later become one of the chief political leaders of Nova Scotia.

The biggest reason that John Sr. stayed in Halifax was that he fell in love. She was a child of a Scottish immigrant from Orkney, Scotland, named Charlotte Pottinger, and they were married on March 24, 1829. The first of their seven children, Mary, was born the following year (named after his mother Mary Sparrow) and their last, John, was born in 1844.

John's actual birth year is a bit of a mystery. He insisted it was November 10, 1844, but baptism records show the year as 1845. Canadian records add to the mystery with some showing 1844 and others sticking with 1845. (This book uses the 1844 date.)

Tragedy strikes

A few years after he was born, tragedy struck the Thompson family. First, his 15-year-old sister, Jane, died in November 1847 and, eight months later, so did his 18-year-old sister, Mary. Both of them died of dropsy—a 17th-century term often found on death certificates to describe some forms of heart failure or kidney disease.

John received his formal education in Halifax at the Royal Acadian School and the Free Church Academy, a Presbyterian grammar school. He was a quiet, somewhat shy youngster who was encouraged by his father to give poetry recitations at school and community events.

As a teenager, John spent much time listening to his father discuss life and politics with friends. His father believed it was every man's duty as a citizen to study politics. The emphasis on politics as a duty stayed with John throughout his life.

Things go terribly wrong

In 1853, his oldest brother, 18-year-old William, was appointed the deputy surveyor of Nova Scotia's Lunenburg County, but things went terribly wrong. He drank, made a mess of his job, and kept such sloppy books that he was investigated for fraud. He lost his job and, in December 1859, went to South Africa, leaving his father to pay back hundreds of British pounds (close to $100,000 today) to cover the alleged fraud.

Besides the emotional pain of his son leaving, William's debt placed a heavy financial burden on the father. So difficult was their situation that his father had to sell the family home—and John, who was not yet 15, was forced to leave school and go to work to help support the family.

He started his first job in September 1860 as a lawyer's apprentice at the law office of Nepean Clarke. The following year, he started articling with a wealthy lawyer and former mayor of Halifax, Henry Pryor. He spent long days on dull work, copying in small, neat writing very lengthy writs, arguments, and pleadings on long pieces of heavy lawyer's paper. He studied

Nova Scotia, diverse from the start

Centuries before Europeans first came to Halifax, the **Mi'kmaq** fished off the shores of what they called *Chebucto* (meaning "biggest harbour"). The Mi'kmaq were a nomadic people, so in the colder weather they would head inland to hunt moose and caribou.

French settlers (later known as Acadians) started to arrive in the 1600s. The Mi'kmaq lived peacefully with them, teaching them how to hunt and fish. The Acadians are famous for the dykes they built to reclaim salt marshes from the sea.

Molly Muise, a well-respected Mi'kmaq woman. This is believed to be the oldest photograph of a Mi'kmaq.

When the British fought for and won control of the land, many Acadians were forced off the land and into exile in the United States. Led by Edward Cornwallis, founder of Halifax, the British weren't much nicer to the Mi'kmaq, who soon found themselves overwhelmed by the number of English, Scottish, and Irish immigrants who arrived. But the British realized that, in order to keep the spot, they had to make some peace with the Mi'kmaq. They did so in a series of peace treaties between 1725 and 1775.

It was the harbour that made Halifax such a desirable location, particularly as a strategic location to fight wars. From the harbour, the British fought many war campaigns, including the **Seven Years' War** (1756–63), the United States War of Independence (1775–1783), the Napoleonic Wars (1799–1815) and the War of 1812

(1812–1814). Over 500,000 Canadian troops left from Halifax to Europe to fight in World War II.

After Great Britain lost against the United States in the War of Independence, people loyal to Britain (**United Empire Loyalists**) left for the remaining British colonies, and many chose Nova Scotia. A large number of loyalists were of African descent, former slaves who fought with the British in return for freedom and land. Many **Black Empire Loyalists** left for Sierra Leone at the first opportunity, upset that the British didn't honour their agreement to treat them respectfully and give them their fair share of land. However, more than two-thirds of the Black Empire Loyalists chose to remain in Nova Scotia where their descendants continue to contribute to the rich cultural heritage of the region.

Halifax used to be an entry port to Canada, particularly between 1921 and 1971. **Pier 21** is a huge building in which immigration officials processed the papers of people from all over the world. Over a million immigrants, refugees, war brides, and children came to Canada via Pier 21 and it is now a museum honouring the many people who started their lives in Canada in its halls.

From Halifax we have Canada's first newspaper (1752), first post office (1755) and first representative assembly (1758).

For more information about Halifax, visit our website at www.jackfruitpress.com.

Annie Affleck, the love of John's life, was the eldest of eight children. Her English-born father, Captain James Affleck, had come to Nova Scotia in 1840 and, four years later, married Newfoundlander Catherine Saunders.

Annie also had two plantation-owning uncles in Barbados, whom her father would visit on his southern voyages.

No one knows what really happened to Captain Affleck; he disappeared and was rumoured to have been lost at sea.

the law thoroughly and did everything in meticulous detail, just as his dad had taught him. Five years later, in 1865, all his hard work paid off—John was admitted to the Nova Scotia **bar** as a full-fledged lawyer.

Things went well until another death struck the Thompson family in 1867. In the summer, his other brother, Joe, died of yellow fever in Texas, where he'd moved with his wife a year earlier. In October—just a few months after Nova Scotia joined **Confederation**—John's father died following a short illness. John, who had been living at the small family home, now became responsible for the sole support of his mother and sister Elizabeth. His other sister, Charlotte, had married a widower from Barrington, Daniel Sargent.

Madly in love

There was one very good thing that happened in John's life around this time—he fell madly in love with the feisty **Annie Affleck**, the free-spirited daughter of a sea captain. Annie was an attractive, witty, high-spirited and intelligent woman but she also had a dark side that would make her moody, irritable, depressed, and fearful of becoming a "useless mope."

Their relationship was not always an easy one—they argued, debated, and fought. But John brought peace to Annie's life and treated her with such gentle, warm kindness that she wrote, "How can I live without it now." When he could not be with her during Christmas 1867, she spent nights staring sadly at the fire and wrote in her diary on December 27, "I felt as if I were all alone in the world, the cold shiver of lonesomeness went over me . . . wondering what I was sent into the world for."

The two became inseparable, with John at Annie's house almost every night. He would teach her French and shorthand he'd learned from his father, or they would simply go for long walks and talk.

John falls madly in love with the feisty Annie Affleck. She's an attractive, witty, high-spirited, and intelligent woman. But she also has a dark side that makes her moody, irritable, and depressed.

Teaching you is no work at all.
I truly enjoy your company.

The two become inseparable. John is at Annie's house almost every night. He teaches her French and the shorthand that he'd learned from his father, or they go for long walks and talk. They become best friends and confidantes.

13

Following in his father's footsteps, John becomes a shorthand reporter for the historic spring session of the 1867 Nova Scotia Assembly (the last session before Confederation).

For the next five years, John supplements his lawyer's income with money he makes as the government's shorthand reporter, transcribing his debate notes late into the night. The next morning, however, he's in his law office, hard at work by 10 a.m.

Chapter 2

A demanding schedule

When John was growing up, his father took three jobs to support the family—and shorthand played a big part in bringing in extra income. Now John followed in his father's footsteps when he became the shorthand reporter for the historic spring session of the 1867 Nova Scotia Assembly (historic because it was the last one before Confederation). For the next five years, John continued to supplement his lawyer's income with a job as the government's shorthand reporter, transcribing debate notes late into the night. The next morning, however, he was hard at work by 10 a.m. in his law office.

It was a demanding schedule and may have contributed to his lifelong poor eating habits. Most days he would lunch at a little restaurant called Wilson's for mutton pie and tea, but the meal gradually became a daily sugar fix of coconut caramels.

In April 1869, he was taken in as a partner by Halifax lawyer Joseph Coombes. At first, John worked behind the scenes while Coombes appeared in court. By 1871, John was appearing in court as well, and

1869
John begins a law partnership with Joseph Coombes.

1870
John and Annie Affleck marry.

1871
John converts to Roman Catholicism.

His first-born daughter dies soon after birth.

John is elected alderman in Halifax city council.

1872
His son, John Thomas, is born.

1874
Son Joseph is born.

1876
Daughter Mary Aloysia is born.

1877
John represents US interests in a fishing dispute involving Canada and Great Britain.

1878
John wins his first election and becomes Nova Scotia's attorney general.

Daughter Mary Helena is born.

1882
John becomes leader of the Nova Scotia Conservatives. He's premier of Nova Scotia for 54 days.

In September 1871, John and Annie's first baby, a daughter, died within an hour of her birth. In 1872, they had a son, John Thomas, and, two years later, a second son, Joseph.

Their daughter, Mary Aloysia, or "Babe" as she was later called, was born in March 1876, followed two years later by Mary Helena, then Frances Alice ("Frankie") in 1881.

John and Annie lost three more kids in the 1880s: Annie Mary (born 1879) died 10 months later, a son died at birth in 1880; and their youngest baby, David Anthony, born in 1883, died in 1885.

In 14 years, Annie had given birth to nine children but had buried four.

the partnership profits were split evenly between the two. They didn't get along, though, and dissolved their partnership in 1873. John continued to practise alone until 1878, when Wallace Graham joined him.

Looking for guidance

There were also changes in John's personal life. After three years of dating, John and Annie were quietly married July 5, 1870, in an American bishop's parlour in Portland, Maine, with Annie's mother present. The newlywed couple then went to live in the Thompson family home with John's mother and sister.

In April 1871, nine months after getting married, John became a Roman Catholic. Born a Methodist, he'd been looking for spiritual direction and guidance since his father died. His decision to convert had been made before marrying Annie, who was born a Catholic, but he waited to announce it. "I did not want it to appear as though I had 'turned' in order to be married."

On September 3, 1871, their first child, a girl, was born, but the infant died within the hour. The following month, while still grieving for their infant daughter, 27-year-old John was elected **alderman** on Halifax city council. His political career had begun.

Into the spotlight

In the spring of 1872—after two years of living with John's mother and sister—John and Annie bought their first home, Willow Park, for an over-priced $12,000. It was a roomy, two-storey frame historical house with two big chimneys, a big verandah, and two acres of surrounding land.

John's work often took him away from the family, but he and Annie continued to write each other daily love letters. Shortly after Joe, their first son, was born, he wrote Annie ". . . and please God as soon as little Joe is weaned we will go right off for about three or four weeks and be 'just married' again."

While still serving as Halifax city councillor, it was fish and the United States that brought John into the spotlight of international politics. He became the central figure in an 1877 multi-million-dollar dispute that pitted Canada and Britain against the United States.

The dispute went back six years, to the 1871 **Treaty of Washington**, when the United States was given fishing rights to the rich inshore fisheries of Canada and Newfoundland. In return, the Canadians got fishing rights in US territorial waters as far south as the 39th parallel. Sound like a fair deal? It did on paper but, in reality, there was a huge problem—the Canadian waters had lots of fish and the US waters did not. Canada and Britain

A demanding work schedule contributes to John's poor eating habits. As these unfortunate habits become a lifelong pattern, John packs on extra pounds.

Most days, he lunches at a little restaurant called Wilson's for mutton pie and tea, but the meals gradually become a daily sugar fix of coconut caramels.

Annie's letters always included stories about the children.

In one letter, she wrote how the kids got "in bed with me last night and they were awake long before daybreak throwing boots at one another and sitting on my head."

Another letter talked about how all the kids had been out in the garden with every coal-oil lamp in the house, trying to make a telephone system.

Such stories tugged deeply at John's heart, like when 5-year-old Babe woke up one morning, wanting to know if her dad would be home by the time she turned 10.

demanded $14.8 million from the United States as compensation for the unfair deal but the Americans refused to pay.

An explosive issue

An international group gathered in Halifax in 1877 to settle the explosive issue. To prepare their case, the Americans looked around for a Canadian lawyer and hired John for a fee of $250 in gold. The three-man tribunal met in Halifax every day for four months. John's skill meant that the US bill was reduced by $9 million; they would only have to pay $5.5 million. To show their appreciation, John's compensation was increased to $750.

While the arbitration was going on, Nova Scotia Conservatives started wooing John to join them. They met with him in October 1877, trying to convince him to enter provincial politics. He declined. Politics didn't interest him; he really wanted to become a judge. But they kept at him until finally he agreed.

John won his first election campaign in 1877, quickly becoming Nova Scotia's leading politician, but found that he didn't like politics. He had to visit his riding in Antigonish every so often. He missed his Annie, his children, and the comforts of home.

A party in trouble

By 1881, John was ready to quit politics. But the Conserative party was in trouble and it did not want him to go. He was very popular, so a powerful Nova Scotian politician, **Sir Charles Tupper**, made a deal with him: if John promised to do his best to lead the Conservatives to another win in the next provincial election, Tupper would appoint him a judge on the Supreme Court of Nova Scotia at the next vacancy. John's goal of becoming a judge was now within reach.

But John couldn't run in the next election with a clear conscience. Everyone knew that he'd be taking the newly vacated seat of the **Nova Scotia Supreme Court**. He actually handed in his resignation letter to Premier Simon Holmes in early May 1882. But Holmes didn't have his party's support and resigned on May 23.

John reluctantly changed his mind and was appointed premier. An election was fast approaching on June 20. Hating the campaigning, John was surprised that he won his seat. The party, however, only won a minority government. John tried to piece together a coalition government but couldn't because everyone knew he was about to resign for the position with the Nova Scotia Supreme Court. He and his **cabinet** resigned in July, 54 days after he became premier.

Law and order: then and now

Before you can become a judge, you need to be a lawyer. But that wasn't always the case. In early Western society, judges were the rich and elite and in 12th-century England, judges would decide guilt or innocence based on "trial by ordeal."

The accused would be ordered to pick up something painful and dangerous, like a red hot bar of iron, or a stone in a cauldron of boiling water. If, after three days, their hands began to heal, they were considered innocent as it proved they had God on their side. Otherwise, they were guilty and the real sentence would be set. Pretty cruel, eh?

Life was less important than property, and people accused of crimes that we'd consider minor now could be sentenced to death. The first recorded death sentence in our part of the world was a 16-year-old girl convicted of petty theft.

By the time that John was a fully trained lawyer, only well-regarded lawyers became judges and guilt or innocence was determined by the facts of a case. John loved the law and felt that it was important and his duty to improve his abilities. John would study legal texts for five hours each night to improve his knowledge of the law.

Sir Charles Tupper appointed John to the Supreme Court of Nova Scotia. Today it is still an appointment process. After 10 years of being a lawyer, you can submit an application, and it is up to a panel (the Judicial Advisory Committee) to decide whether or not your application will get you onto the provincial judiciary. When a spot becomes available on the nine-member federal **Supreme Court** team, it is up to the prime minister to choose a judge to fill the position.

According to Ontario Judge Marvin Morten, one of the key differences between being a judge now and being one in Sir John's time is that, back then, judges focused on punishment. Punishments were quite harsh and included death by hanging and whipping.

These days, many judges find ways of interacting with the community to ensure that they really understand the values of the communities they serve. Some go into schools to give talks, mentor students, or serve breakfast at homeless shelters.

Today's judges focus on: ensuring a trial is fair; deterrents (ways of preventing crime); and, in terms of young people in particular, rehabilitation (helping people who have done something wrong learn to live in society again so that they're unlikely to commit crimes again).

No, it's not Santa Claus: this is the Right Honourable Beverley McLachlin, P. C. Chief Justice of Canada, wearing the traditional robes of her prestigious role. She is Canada's top judge, appointed by Prime Minister Chrétien in 2000.

For more information about judges, visit our website at www.jackfruitpress.com.

Determined to be well-educated and knowledgeable, John reads law every day for five hours. He believes in legal excellence for fighting injustice and wants to find a better way to educate not only himself, but all lawyers in Nova Scotia.

In 1883, John becomes one of the founders of Dalhousie University's law school, the first university law faculty in Canada outside of Quebec. One of his favourite jobs is teaching students of the new faculty.

Chapter 3

Mr. Justice Thompson

John was appointed a Nova Scotia Supreme Court judge on July 24, 1882. His legal arguments were orderly and easy to understand. This gained him an impressive reputation as a judge on the Supreme Court of Nova Scotia. Determined to be a well-educated and knowledgeable judge, John made a resolution to read law every day for five hours.

In the late 1800s, fewer than one in four Nova Scotia lawyers had a university degree. Like John, they went from public school to being a lawyer's apprentice. John believed in legal excellence in fighting injustice and wanted to find a better way to educate not only himself, but all lawyers in Nova Scotia. So, in 1883, he became one of the founders of the Dalhousie Law School, the first university law faculty in Canada outside of Quebec.

Part of John's job as minister of justice was to consider requests from people who thought their trials were unfair.

Although he judged that Louis Riel should hang for his part in the Red River and Northwest rebellions, he let a number of the others involved in the incidents go free.

However, he had absolutely no sympathy if a crime had anything to do with cruelty to children. When a woman who had mistreated a two-year-old asked for mercy, John said, "I tell you, if I lived for 100 years and I was still minister of justice, you would never get out with my consent!"

At the new law school, John lectured on evidence and talked a lot about his experiences in criminal law. While a judge, John modernized and simplified the day-to-day administration of the Nova Scotia Supreme Court during the winter of 1883–1884. He did such a great job that, except for minor adjustments, the massive document of 160 printed pages remained in force for the next 66 years, until 1950.

John enjoyed being a judge, but destiny was calling. In July 1885, Prime Minister Macdonald asked him to join federal politics as the minister of justice. John left the decision to Annie—he would do whatever she wanted him to do. She told him to accept Macdonald's offer. She could see his potential for greatness and knew he would make an exceptional statesman. On September 2, 1885, he officially agreed to join the federal cabinet.

As a cabinet minister, John made $7,000 a year (almost double the $4,000 he'd been making as a judge). And as a growing family, they sure did need the money. Just that summer, they'd sent their eldest son, John, to England to attend college, knowing Joseph would follow later.

As a new federal minister, one of John's first social invitations was to dine with Prime Minister Macdonald and Lady Macdonald at Earnscliffe, their dark, somewhat sombre, home. The dinner was typical for the wealthy in Ottawa—"oysters, consommé, fish, lamb cutlets, cabinet pudding, *charlotte russe*, lemon ice, and fruit."

Lonely and depressed

The Thompsons couldn't afford two residences and they weren't ready to part with their first home, so Annie continued to live with the children at Willow Park in Nova Scotia, while John lived in two-room apartment in a boarding house about a 10-minute walk from **Parliament Hill**. John missed his family and was still not convinced they had made the right decision. He wrote Annie, "I could not stand the depression so long as this but for the feeling all the time that you wished me to do what I have done."

When John joined the cabinet in 1885, it was an extremely tense time in Canadian history. **Louis Riel**—the leader of a provisional government in what is now Manitoba, defender of **Métis** and **First Nations** rights, and leader of the 1885 Northwest Rebellion—had been sentenced to death as a traitor, even though the jury had put in a recommendation for mercy. The original date of execution had been set for September 2, but it kept getting postponed due to appeals. Public pressure had been building to get the government to have Riel spend the rest of his life in prison instead.

John joins the federal cabinet as Louis Riel—the Métis rebel leader—is sentenced to death as a traitor. The date of his execution keeps getting postponed as public pressure builds to have Riel spend his life in prison instead.

John's wife, Annie, gives him this advice: "Let Riel go to prison . . . if you hang him, you make a patriot of him." As for Riel, he feels no anger about his execution. Before he's hanged on November 16, he's reported to have said, "Sir John Macdonald is now committing me to death for the same reason I committed Scott—because it is necessary for this country's good."

Louis Riel was a Métis lawyer who was thrust into Canadian history when he stood on a chain (used by government surveyors to measure his cousin's farm) and ordered them off the property.

He led two armed rebellions against the Canadian government: the Red River Rebellion in 1869 and the Northwest Rebellion in 1885.

He was fighting for the rights and lands of the Métis and other First Nations peoples in the areas that later became Manitoba and Saskatchewan. They'd asked him to help out after Confederation, fearing that their lands would be taken away by European settlers.

The hanging of Louis Riel

Annie wrote to John saying she did not want to see Riel hanged. "Let Riel go to prison…if you hang him you make a patriot of him. If you send him to prison, he is only an insane man." She added that, if he must hang, not to let it happen on November 10 because that was John's birthday.

Riel was hanged on November 16 in Regina at the **North West Mounted Police** headquarters. Riel held no anger at Macdonald for refusing to stop his execution and was reported to have said, "Sir John Macdonald is now committing me to death for the same reason I committed [**Thomas**] **Scott**—because it is necessary for this country's good."

Debating the death sentence

When Parliament opened on February 25, 1886, John walked into a **House of Commons** that was primed for a hot debate over the execution of Louis Riel. As minister of justice, the nation expected him to defend the government's actions.

It started when a Quebec Conservative **member of Parliament** (MP) for Montmagny, A. G. P. R. Landry, moved on March 11 "…that this House feels it is its duty to express its deep grief that the sentence of death passed upon Louis Riel, convicted of high treason, was allowed to be carried into execution."

The debate continued for days. On March 19, **Liberal** Opposition Leader **Edward Blake** made a five-hour speech denouncing the government during which, alas, most of his followers fell asleep. Three days later, it was the government's turn, setting the stage for John's first major speech in Parliament. Could he pull it off or would he embarrass the government?

On Monday, March 22, the **visitors' galleries** were packed with people, all wanting to see if John could defend the government's decision to hang Riel. John stood up at 4 p.m. and started his speech. For the next four hours, in a loud, clear voice, he focused on the core question in Landry's motion: should Riel have been executed.

A war of extermination

He told the members of Parliament, that "Riel was fairly tried, honestly convicted, laudably condemned, and justly executed." He talked about Riel instigating the rebellion murders, including the 1885 massacre at Frog Lake. And he reminded the House that, just before the Duck Lake murders, Riel had shouted at a Scottish Métis, Thomas McKay, "It is blood. We want blood. It is a war of extermination. Everybody that is against us is to be driven out of the country."

Thompson's criminal code: a model for the world

Crime used to be considered a personal matter, something that the victim's family could sort out with the family of the offender. But this has changed; now we look to police, lawyers, and judges to help us when we're wronged.

We can thank Sir John for Canada's first **criminal code**: the book that describes all the ways you can break the law in Canada. It also describes the ways to punish people for breaking the law. The criminal code is a major achievement in Canadian legal history. Sir John took the lead in writing and developing the code, which was based on "The Stephen Code," an 1878 model written by Sir James Fitzjames Stephen. But Sir James's version was never approved by English parliament.

Both Sir John and Sir James had the same philosophy: crime is not only wrong and should be punished, but should be seen to be punished. Back in John's time, use of balls and chains were public displays that you were a criminal and were used to make sure that criminals could not run away.

The Canadian Criminal Code is a federal law that applies to every part of Canada. It defines what a crime is, the criminal procedures that apply to it, and the range of punishments if convicted. What does that really mean? Basically, you can't be convicted of a criminal offence if it isn't specifically written in the criminal code.

Before Canadian Confederation in 1867, each province had its own criminal law, based on the English system. After Confederation, Canada's first prime minister, Sir John A. Macdonald, pushed for one criminal code in Canada, one that applied to every part of the land. So, in the new constitution, the federal government was the only authority given power to develop a criminal code and organize it into a code or system. It was left to the provinces, though, to administer the criminal-law justice system.

Macdonald died a year before Parliament passed the Canadian Criminal Code, the world's first complete codification.

For example, the code specified that stealing potatoes was a crime and that one of the punishments could be whipping. The code states that "whenever whipping may be awarded for any offence . . . the number of strokes shall be specified in the sentence and the instrument to be used shall be a cat-o'-nine-tails unless some instrument is specified in the sentence. Whipping shall not be inflicted on any female."

As the example shows, with changing times, Thompson's code has also had to be changed. What would he have thought of the types of crimes we have today, like terrorism, gun crimes and drunk-driving offences? But at least there aren't as many horse rustlers as there were in Sir John's time, eh?

For more information about criminal codes, visit our website at www.jackfruitpress.com.

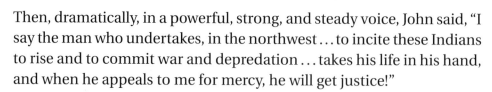

John just kept winning elections, often to his own surprise. As we know, he really wanted to be a judge and live closer to his family in Nova Scotia.

He did not like campaigning and felt that crowds were always at the "boiling point" making a real discussion impossible. He wanted to leave politics.

He found Sundays in Ottawa particularly difficult. He would wander the streets and peer into the houses, where he could see men with their wives and children. This made him sad as his were so far away.

Annie urged him to stay. But John could not do without his family and finally they moved to Ottawa, too.

Then, dramatically, in a powerful, strong, and steady voice, John said, "I say the man who undertakes, in the northwest … to incite these Indians to rise and to commit war and depredation … takes his life in his hand, and when he appeals to me for mercy, he will get justice!"

Exceptional praise

His party members, and even some Liberals, cheered loudly. The next day, the *Montreal Star* called his speech "by long odds the most powerful argument yet made for government." And the Toronto *Globe*'s parliamentary correspondent, S. Willison, gave him exceptional praise.

> When he [Thompson] sat down after his first [major] speech in the House of Commons, it was realized that a great figure had emerged from a curious obscurity. From the first, he commanded its interest and confidence. He was simple, lucid, persuasive, and convincing. He seemed to be interested only in the logical structure of the argument. In short, he gave an impression of simplicity, sincerity, and integrity, and in Parliament these are the qualities that prevail.

It wasn't long after this speech that Ottawa was abuzz: would Thompson be the successor to the aging Prime Minister Macdonald?

Moving to Ottawa

After his re-election in the 1887 general election (he still represented Antigonish County), John and Annie began to talk about moving the family to Ottawa the following year.

In the summer of 1887, soon after the **parliamentary session** ended, Thompson headed to Nova Scotia with his cousin, David Pottinger, to see his ailing mother. He wrote Annie, "I should go to see her as it will be the last time I shall have the chance." He was right. She died on July 9, 1887, surrounded by her surviving children—John, Elizabeth, and Charlotte. After his mother's funeral, John returned to Ottawa … and to work.

John A. Macdonald put John in charge of the government so that he could escape the Ottawa summer heat. This meant that John had to go to all the political meetings that took place in the Ottawa area. One meeting lasted for six hours on a day when it was 34°C in the shade.

With John away most of the year, Annie has to care for everything at home in Halifax. She's lonely, worries about having enough money, gains weight, and gets depressed.

Halifax

Ottawa

She also writes a lot of letters. On a typical day, she writes a letter to John in the morning, at noon, and in the evening. John is struggling with loneliness too. Having returned to Ottawa after spending Christmas at home, he writes: "Transplanting a man like me is very hard work." Annie replies, "Oh my Pet my Pet, Baby you break my heart . . . look this thing in the face and make the best of it for a little while until I can be with you."

1886

A thorny fishing debate heats up when Canada arrests the US schooner *David J. Adams* and, later, the *Ella M. Doughty* for fishing violations. The Americans are furious, with one US newspaper calling Canada's actions "unlawful and unfriendly."

The US congress gives President Grover Cleveland the power to cut off all trade with Canada if the seizures of the Adams and Doughty are not resolved to US satisfaction.

Chapter 4

Confronting the Americans

For years, fishing rights and treaties were quarrelsome issues among Canada, Great Britain, and the United States. But things really began to heat up when, in May 1886, Canada arrested the US schooner *David J. Adams* and then, later, the *Ella M. Doughty*, both for fishing violations. The United States was furious, with one US newspaper calling Canada's actions "unlawful" and "unfriendly." US president Grover Cleveland was given power by **congress** to cut off all trade with Canada if the seizures of the *Adams* and *Doughty* were not resolved to US satisfaction. But Cleveland's secretary of state, a reasonable and intelligent man, suggested that negotiating would be better. A high commission of representatives from Canada, the United States, and Great Britain met in Washington in November 1887.

1887
John assists Charles Tupper in negotiating a settlement to the century-old fishing dispute between Britain, the former colonies of British North America (now Canada), and the United States.

1888
John is knighted by Queen Victoria for his work solving the fisheries dispute.

The Thompsons move to Ottawa.

1889
Sir John acts to protect the Canadian book-publishing industry by developing a new Canadian Copyright Act.

1891
Prime Minister Macdonald dies.

1892
Sir John becomes Canada's fourth prime minister.

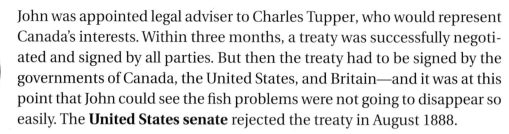

Macaroni and cheese wasn't on the menu when, two times a week, Sir John and Annie held dinner parties for MPs and their wives.

These parties were part of John's responsibilities as a cabinet minister, but he and Annie sure did find it difficult to pay for and prepare so much food.

And, boy, could those hungry ministers pack it away! A typical menu would consist of oysters, consommé, fish, lamb cutlets, cabinet pudding, *charlotte russe*, lemon ice, and fruit.

For 20 people, two times a week, that would cost over $46,000 a year today—and back then it would have gobbled up a hefty portion of Sir John's salary.

John was appointed legal adviser to Charles Tupper, who would represent Canada's interests. Within three months, a treaty was successfully negotiated and signed by all parties. But then the treaty had to be signed by the governments of Canada, the United States, and Britain—and it was at this point that John could see the fish problems were not going to disappear so easily. The **United States senate** rejected the treaty in August 1888.

Luckily, a clause was included in the treaty to deal with the Senate rejecting it. Called a *modus vivendi*, the Canadians charged American fishermen a licensing fee per ton of fish caught in Canadian waters.

The dropout gets knighted

John's legal work in the fishing negotiations was so outstanding that, in August 1888—to his surprise—Queen Victoria awarded him the Knight Commander, Order of St. Michael and St. George (KCMG). Sounds fancy. What it meant was that Britain had given John a **knighthood**. He was now Sir John David Thompson, and his wife Annie, the Lady Anne Thompson. Who could have imagined it—a school dropout from Nova Scotia receiving a knighthood? **John Allison Bell**, from Halifax, wrote in his diaries, "What would his good old father think, or what does he think of all this, if watching from loopholes of the other world?"

Meanwhile, in March 1888, the Thompson family had finally moved to Ottawa. The Thompson's Nova Scotia home, Willow Park, was boarded up and left unattended because John couldn't bear to sell it.

Before long, Sir John and Annie were entertaining in Ottawa in a manner expected of a federal cabinet minister. It was a demanding and expensive task, with dinner parties for about 20 people every Monday and Tuesday. They would serve a feast for members of Parliament and their wives. Later, when finances got tight, Annie had to do all the cooking by herself.

Sir John enjoyed having his beloved Annie and seven-year-old daughter Frankie with him in Ottawa. Frankie would come to the gallery of the House of Commons with Annie and throw kisses at her father below.

Their other four children were away at school: John and Joe in England and daughters Babe and Helena north of Montreal at Sacred Heart Convent in Sault aux Récollets. Sir John wanted them to be fluent in French because he felt being bilingual would "be very important in Canada."

The death of Macdonald

Around the same time, Sir John was dealing with the smouldering distrust between French and English Canadians. This time it was sparked by Quebec's passing of the **Jesuit Estates Act**, a law that compensated Jesuit priests for properties seized by Great Britain when it was awarded the colony of New France in 1763 at the end of the Seven Years' War. France

Relations with the United States

Although it sometimes seems otherwise, Canada and the United States are pretty good friends and neighbours. We're able to work together and visit each other easily. Some of our communities are located right on the border (there are even homes that are half in Canada and half in the United States). This would be unthinkable in many parts of the world, but rarely causes any problems here. Overall, our relationship is considered one of the best there possibly can be between two nations.

Relations between our two countries was not very good at the beginning—during Confederation, terrorists were using the United States as a base to launch attacks into Canada—and, until the 1940s, Canada's military was figuring out ways to stop a possible US invasion. Gradually, relations improved, and many agreements were made to improve trade and resolve problems.

In World War I and II, Canada and the United States were allies, fighting together in Europe and Asia. Afterward, our two countries strengthened their military alliance to oppose the Soviet Union in what is known as the Cold War. At the same time, we have become more similar culturally, with Canadians watching US movies and TV shows, which often star Canadian celebrities.

But we also have many disputes, on a wide range of issues. Many of them involve trade, which is not surprising as Canada sends most of its goods south to the United States. Another long-standing problem is that the United States rejects Canadian claims over parts of the far north, particularly over waterways between islands in the Arctic.

Dealing with the United States is one of the biggest challenges any prime minister can face. Pierre Trudeau once said, "Living next to you is in some ways like sleeping with an elephant. No matter how friendly and even-tempered is the beast, if I can call it that, one is affected by every twitch and grunt." Jean Chrétien neatly summed up his position on the United States during a private conversation. "I like to stand up to the Americans. It's popular," he said. Afterward he added, "you have to be very careful because they're our friends."

Chrétien didn't know that his words were overheard by a nearby microphone, which allowed the media to hear him too. Canadians like to show some anti-Americanism, but that kind of opposition can only go so far, because no one wants to make an enemy out of the world's most powerful nation.

Americans also have their own views of Canadians; sometimes they're not very flattering. Often they see us as preachy and smug, not nearly conservative enough, and they believe we think we're smarter than them.

For more information about US–Canada relations, visit our website at www.jackfruitpress.com.

While the French and English continued to duke it out, Sir John learned, from a secret agent sent to New York, that a small but noisy section of the Liberal party wanted to help the United States take over Canada.

Sir John realized it was a small but real conspiracy. It didn't involve Liberal party leader Wilfrid Laurier, but it did include Quebec premier Honoré Mercier (the guy on the next page).

This helped convince him that Canada needed Great Britain's protection and that it wasn't quite ready to be independent.

surrendered New France to Great Britain. French-Canadian Catholics feared losing their religion, culture, and language. English Canadians felt the French Canadians were to be assimilated into the English culture. And it didn't help when, in 1889, Quebec's Premier **Honoré Mercier** called on French Canadians to fight the threat of an Anglo-Saxon world.

Thompson took no sides, supporting instead the idea that the cultures and nationalities of both the French and English could coexist in one united Canada. When MPs in Ottawa tried to have the provincial act cancelled, John gave a powerful speech in the House of Commons to say that this troubling issue that included religion and race was between the Quebec government and the Catholic church. And, if Confederation was going to succeed, it would take Catholics and Protestants, French and English, getting along. Furthermore, the federal government must not interfere with the provincial legislatures while they govern in ways that are appropriate for their people.

Sir John was very sad when Prime Minister Macdonald died in June 1891. It was not an unexpected death—everyone knew that the prime minister was quite ill—but it's always hard to lose an old friend. The whole nation mourned the passing of the "old rascal." Sir John said, "there is not one of us who has not lost his heart to him."

The **governor general** asked Sir John Abbot to be prime minister, although everybody knew that it was really John who ruled in the House of Commons. When Abbot resigned due to ill health in November 1892, Sir John became prime minister at age 48.

John becomes prime minister

His first speech as prime minister was on January 5, 1893, at a **Board of Trade** dinner in Toronto. As he rose to speak, the audience gave him a standing ovation and listened intently as he spoke about Canadian nationhood. "The country ought to be a nation, will be a nation, and, please God, we will and shall make it a nation."

Thompson was a nationalist, but strongly opposed immediate independence from Great Britain. He said that to even suggest it was "to talk absurdity, if not treason." He felt Canada still needed the protection of the **British Empire** to safeguard it from being taken over by the United States. There was no doubt in his mind that someday Canada would be a totally independent sovereign nation, but that time was not now.

John knows that French- and English-speaking Canadians are at odds with each other. French Canadians fear losing their religion, culture, and language while English Canadians hope assimilation can occur in a couple of generations.

Religious intolerance is sparked when Quebec premier Honoré Mercier makes a passionate St-Jean-Baptiste Day speech urging French Canadians to fight English assimilation. John wisely takes no sides, supporting instead the idea that both cultures and nationalities can flourish in one united Canada.

1894

Three separate doctors examine John and reach different conclusions. One says John has heart disease. Another says he needs to lose weight. A third insists there's nothing wrong and predicts he'll live another 30 years.

CANADIAN NATIONAL EXHIBITION GATE 2

As the parliamentary session ends, Sir John is absolutely exhausted. When his wife and son join him in Toronto to celebrate Canada's first Labour Day at the Canadian National Exhibition, he doesn't suspect that they've come to keep an eye on his health.

34

Chapter 5

Stretched and stressed

1893

John, Annie, and their three daughters join son Joe in Europe.

John is appointed a judge on the Bering Sea Tribunal.

The Bering Sea Tribunal decides that Canadians have the right to hunt seals in the Bering Sea.

John is called to the Imperial Privy Council.

Lord Aberdeen becomes governor general of Canada.

1894

Everyone is worried about John's health. John worries about money.

Canada's first Labour Day holiday takes place.

In the early 1890s, Canada was in a mess. The economy was sinking into recession and Canadians were moving to the United States by the hundreds of thousands.

One of Sir John's first duties as prime minister was to help solve the marine problem that was still brewing between Canada and the United States. This time, it was Canada that was outraged over the arrest of its boats. Also, this renewed dispute was over seals, not fish. Sir John headed to Europe to work with others to find a diplomatic way to solve the problem. The key question facing them was whether the United States had the right to seize 17 Canadian sealing ships in the Bering Sea between 1886 and 1890.

Joining Sir John on this European trip was his wife, Annie, and their three daughters. Son Joe, still in England, was going to meet them in Paris (eldest son John was in Toronto, working as a lawyer's apprentice). The Thompsons left for France in March 1893, on the French steamer *La Bretagne*.

Five months later, on August 15, the **Bering Sea Tribunal**'s decision was announced in Paris and it was all good news for Canada: the

Back in the 1880s, women still didn't have the right to vote. John thought they should have the same rights as men.

Had John been in power longer, Canadian women probably would have won the right to vote in federal elections much earlier than they did.

It wasn't until 1917 that this changed. Two thousand military nurses were the first Canadian women to vote when the government allowed female British subjects who were active members of the Canadian Forces to vote. Women with a close relative serving in the Forces could also vote.

In 1918, all women 21 years and over were eligible to vote.

United States had no right to seize the Canadian ships. Three years later, an agreement between the two countries was reached to pay for the 17 ships left to rot on Alaskan beaches and in harbours. The United States paid almost $500,000. Sir John was rewarded for the successful ruling from the Bering Sea Tribunal. He was called to the Imperial **Privy Council**—an honour that entitled him to have "Right Honourable" in front of his name.

When Sir John returned to Ottawa on August 26, 1893, he had gained more weight, perhaps from the fine French cuisine. There was a touch of foreboding when he wrote to his son Joe, who was vacationing in the south of France with the rest of the family. "When I saw you in Paris, I was quite glad to see what a man you had become . . . keep care of your mother and the children. You are a fine big fellow now and will be able to take my place."

Standing up for women's rights

Back in Canada, Sir John's passion for fairness and justice turned now to women's issues. Sir John made it clear where he stood on the subject. In September 1893 he said, "We look forward to it as one of the aims which are to be accomplished in the public life of Canada, because the Conservative party believes that the influence of women in the politics of the country is always for good." Had Sir John lived, women in Canada probably would have been given the right to vote much sooner than they were.

It was also in September that pioneering feminist, **Lady Aberdeen**, arrived in Ottawa from England with her husband, the Earl of Aberdeen, the new governor general of Canada. The Aberdeens were a remarkable couple, both well-educated, modest, and hard-working. **Lord Aberdeen** was John Hamilton Gordon, a gentle man with a passion for trains and horses; Lady Aberdeen was Ishbel Marjoribanks, a confident, intense, vigorous woman.

Within a month of arriving in Canada, Lady Aberdeen made a rousing speech about women's issues to 1,500 women gathered in Toronto to start the **National Council of Women** (NCW). Not only did Sir John support Lady Aberdeen's fiery feminist views, but he and Annie became close friends with the Lady and Lord Aberdeen.

Struggling with money

On the home front, the Thompsons continued to struggle financially, trying not to go broke on the prime minister's annual salary of $9,000. Early in 1894, they were renting a house when the landlord offered to sell it to them for $11,000. John declined, explaining he simply could not afford it.

Their family finances were stretched to the limit because of their children's medical and education costs. In April 1894, Sir John wrote a friend in Halifax, "I am somewhat short of money." The same month, he wrote

Getting on the wrong side of your parents . . . and going to jail

Can you imagine being sent to a reformatory for yelling at your parents? Hard to believe now, but at one time it was a crime.

The 19th-century Canadian legal system allowed parents, tired of supporting rebellious children, to bring their kids to a magistrate and have them convicted of frivolous offences and sent to kids' jail, known then as a reformatory. Bet you've heard of "reform school." Well, there was not much difference between it and a jail back then.

In 1880, the province of Ontario even passed a law that a parent or guardian of any boy between 10 and 13 years old could arrange to have him sent to a reformatory for up to five years if a judge deemed the boy beyond control.

Sir John felt there was never a justification for such action and it angered him. In a terse letter to Mr. Justice Rose of Ontario Court of Common Pleas, he voiced his indignation about how the legal system was catering to the demands of parents abandoning their parental roles. He cited a case where a boy was sentenced to five years in penitentiary for wearing an article of clothing belonging to his father and another where a boy was sent to the notoriously brutal St. Vincent Penitentiary for taking a few cents from his brother's pant pockets.

Sir John wrote that many parents seemed "to think the Reformatory is a place for supporting and training their children. In such circumstances, I look upon the parents as guilty of a heinous crime . . . and the magistrate is often their accessory and under such circumstances I would not hesitate to order a release, no matter what the warden thinks of the boy's condition and program."

Sir John had strong words for those like Senator **Oliver Mowat** from Ontario, who seemed to think it was all right that young boys could be imprisoned at the will of a warden. He said, "If we come to that in this country, it will be better that such penal institutions be abolished by legislature or even destroyed as instruments of evil."

He had a passion for justice for young offenders and put in safeguards for them when he wrote the Canadian Criminal Code, passed by Parliament in 1892. It established, for example, that children under the age of 14 could not be charged unless they understood they had committed a crime and could understand that it was wrong. Also, young offenders under 16 years of age must be tried without publicity.

This is Albert Turner, age 9, in 1872, England. He was sentenced to 14 days of hard labour and four years in reformatory for stealing watches.

For more information about young offenders, visit our website at www.jackfruitpress.com.

his brother-in-law, James A. Chisholm, to ask if he could postpone payment on a debt. "I am abominably hard up just now and will be so for a few weeks," he said.

Some politicians, like Sir Charles Tupper, who noted that Sir John had only one winter coat and a single pair of gloves, thought Thompson had financially ruined his family by being too honest and refusing to accept money for political favours. Even Prime Minister Macdonald was rumoured to have taken election funds for his personal use (he died leaving $200,000 to his widow). However, for Sir John, such pilfering was unthinkable. Lady Aberdeen wrote in her journal, "And Sir John's honesty was scrupulous . . . No **public moneys** have ever found their way to his pocket."

A live coward or a dead hero?

By the time the 1894 parliamentary session ended, Sir John was absolutely exhausted and pushing himself physically to the limit. One colleague wrote to him in early August, "All I hope is, old man, that you feel better and better every day and that you are really resting."

Sir John did briefly rest, spending August with his family in the Muskokas, but he was back at work on Canada's first **Labour Day** on September 3, 1894, a holiday he had pushed to create. A couple of days later, Annie and son John met him in Toronto for the opening of the 1894 Canadian National Exhibition. Annie wasn't there to see the festivities but to keep an eye on Sir John's health. He felt sick and had swelling in his legs.

Sir John visited doctors in Toronto, Ottawa, and Montreal. One said he found evidence of **Bright's disease** and heart disease. Another said John's heart was sound but he needed to lose weight. A third said there was nothing seriously wrong and predicted John would live another 30 years.

Annie and his friends continued to be worried. In Halifax, **Bishop Cameron** (who loved Sir John as a son) was so uneasy about the haggard look of his long-time friend that he said a mass for him on September 29. The bishop told Lady Aberdeen that, of all the men he'd ever known, Sir John seemed to him the one who lived with "…a sense of the presence of God about him."

Another team of doctors examined Thompson in late September and recommended he give up work for a year. For the first time in their married life, Annie urged her husband to stop and immediately resign as prime minister…but he said it would be cowardly of him. She told him, "I would rather have a live coward than a dead hero." He refused. He felt it was his duty to lead the Conservatives through the next election in 1895, promising he would leave politics if they won.

Many Canadian politicians didn't hesitate to profit from the public purse. Some became rich at the expense of Canadian taxpayers.

John wasn't like that. He was scrupulously honest, even if it meant that his family experienced a lot of hardship because of it.

On the home front, the Thompsons continue to struggle financially, trying not to go broke on the prime minister's annual salary. Their family finances are stretched to the limit because of the childen's ongoing medical and education costs.

Some politicians, like Sir Charles Tupper, think that John is financially ruining his family by being too honest and refusing to accept money for political favours. However, for Sir John, taking money from the public purse is unthinkable.

1894

Travelling to London on government business, John meets up with his daughter, Helena. John and Helena have fun touring Europe—until he becomes breathless after climbing to the top of St. Peter's Basilica in Rome.

Helena accompanies her father back to London. Sir John goes right back to work at the Canadian High Commission but, within hours, returns to the hotel, breathless and feeling ill. He sees a doctor, who tells him he has strained his heart and should be careful. Feeling better after a three-day rest, he returns to his hectic pace.

Chapter 6

One last trip abroad

1894
October
John sails to England to be sworn in to the Imperial Privy Council.

December
John works at the Canadian High Commission.

December 11
John dines with Charles Tupper.

December 12
John faints at his swearing-in ceremony. Soon after, he suffers a fatal heart attack.

December 21
Sir Mackenzie Bowell becomes the fifth prime minister of Canada.

December 22
The ship carrying John's body leaves for Canada.

1885
January 1
John's body arrives in Halifax.

January 3
He's buried in Holy Cross Cemetery.

1913
His wife, Annie, dies.

In late fall of 1894, Prime Minister Thompson was called to England to tackle a number of issues and to be officially sworn in as a member of Her Majesty's Privy Council, the second Canadian after Sir John A. Macdonald to be so honoured. He also planned to spend some time with his daughter, Helena, who was attending school in Paris. On a cold, rainy October 31, Annie and Frankie said goodbye to Sir John as he sailed out from New York aboard the steamer *Majestic*.

At first, things went well for Sir John. He had a great time with Helena, touring Europe until he became breathless after climbing to the top of St. Peter's Basilica in Rome. Helena came back to London, England, with her father on Saturday, December 1. Sir John went right back to work at the Canadian **High Commission** but, within hours, returned to the hotel, breathless and not feeling well. He visited a doctor who told him he'd strained his heart and that he should be careful.

Suddenly, without a sound

After three days, he felt better and continued his hectic pace. On Tuesday evening, December 11, after bidding farewell to Helena as she returned to Paris, he had supper with Sir Charles Tupper, the Canadian high commissioner, then returned to his hotel at about 11 p.m.

The next day, Sir John took a train to Windsor Castle for his swearing-in ceremony. The 20-minute ceremony started at 1:15 p.m. and was followed by lunch in the Octagon Room. Then things started to go horribly wrong.

Sir John fainted before he even touched his food. He was helped to a nearby private writing room where he sat down, put his head in his hands and, after a bit of water and brandy, seemed to recover. Embarrassed at having caused such a scene, he remarked, "It seems too weak and foolish to faint like this."

Then, cheerfully, he announced, "I'm all right now, thank you," walking back into the dining room unaided. In the meantime, Queen Victoria had sent for her own physician, Dr. Reid, who arrived just as Sir John was being seated to lunch. Dr. Reid sat beside him. Suddenly, without a sound, Sir John collapsed against the doctor.

Dr. Reid quickly put some him brandy to his lips and reached over to check his pulse. But there was nothing the doctor could do. Sir John Thompson was already dead.

A formal state funeral

The British admiralty brought back Sir John's body in the HMS *Blenheim,* one of the newest and fastest cruisers of the British navy. The black-painted vessel left England on December 22 for the 10-day sea voyage to Halifax. It was timed to arrive at noon on a rainy January 1, 1895.

Solemn music played as Sir John's body was escorted off the ship to the steam launch for the short trip to the landing. On shore, the body was placed on a gun carriage and covered with the Red Ensign flag. Four black horses pulled the carriage through the rain as the King's Band played the Death March. They stopped at Province House, and there Sir John's body lay in state in the Red Room Legislative Council chamber.

Devastated by her husband's death, Annie told her friend Lady Aberdeen she despaired "never to hear his voice again, never to hear him come in at the door, never to hear him come up the stairs again—never, never—oh! I am afraid of the nights and I am afraid of the days and am afraid of the years and if it were not for the children, I should long to creep away in some corner and die."

John was the only Canadian PM whose funeral involved a royal ship. His body was brought home on a ship that had its sides painted black for the occasion..

Sir John is in Windsor Castle, in England. It is Wednesday, December 12, and he is about to be sworn in as the Right Honourable Sir John Thompson. The 20-minute ceremony starts at 1:15 p.m. and is followed by lunch in the Octagon Room.

He faints before he even touches his food, but seems to recover. Queen Victoria sits him beside her own doctor. Then, suddenly, without a sound, Sir John collapses and dies. There is nothing the doctor can do—Sir John has had a fatal heart attack.

When you lose a leader as brilliant and dedicated as John, how can you possibly replace him?

Well, sometimes you can't.

Mackenzie Bowell, John's successor as PM, was a dud. As historian Gordon Donaldson has said, Bowell "is remembered, if at all, as a stupid, bigoted, conceited, and slightly paranoiac little man."

The funeral was held on Thursday, January 3, in St. Mary's Cathedral. Over 7,000 people had applied for a place in the 700-seat church. Following Mass, the funeral procession slowly made its way the half mile to Holy Cross Cemetery. Sir John was buried in the family plot, surrounded by the graves of his three young children, Annie's mother, and her two brothers.

Sir John had around $24,000 when he'd died, which was not enough money for Annie to live on. To keep Annie from being destitute, the government established the Lady Thompson Fund and raised $62,500, which was invested to provide a lifelong income of approximately $2,800 a year (which would be like $70,000 today).

30 trunks of papers

After his death, Annie and Frankie moved to Toronto, along with over 30 trunks of Sir John's papers, which Annie had meticulously saved over the years. Long before his death, she'd recognized the historical importance of these documents. Year after year, she'd filled boxes with his letters and papers. Included were family and official correspondence.

Annie lived in Toronto until her death on April 10, 1913. In 1949, after 55 years in the Thompson family, the 30 trunks of Thompson papers were brought to the public archives (now Library and Archives Canada) by the Thompson's eldest son, Colonel John Thomas Thompson.

If it hadn't been for the dedication and foresight of Annie, a valuable part of Canadian history could well have been lost forever. Sir John's legacy lives on, thanks in large measure to his beloved Lady Annie Thompson.

The British admiralty brings back Sir John's body in the HMS *Blenheim*, one of the newest and fastest cruisers of the British navy. After 10 days at sea, the black-painted ship arrives in Halifax at noon on a rainy January 1.

Sir John's body is escorted off the ship to the steam launch, then placed on a gun carriage and covered with the Red Ensign flag. Four black horses pull the carriage behind the King's Band while funeral music plays all the way to Province House. Devastated by her husband's death, Annie tells her friend "If it were not for the children, I would long to creep away in some corner and die."

Sir John S. D. Thompson

"Would that I had the opportunity to do more for the well-being of this great land called Canada."

Sir John S. D. Thompson

Many famous people have gone on record saying that Sir John Thompson could have been one of Canada's greatest prime ministers. But, as we already know, he didn't have much chance to demonstrate his potential.

His accomplishments are many

There's no doubt that John left an important legacy. His accomplishments are many. He negotiated important fishing treaties between Canada and the United States, helping to bring peace between two squabbling countries. He was an out-standing lawyer and a co-founder of Nova Scotia's famous Dalhousie Law School. He also spear-headed the creation of the Canadian Criminal Code, the first such code in the world. He campaigned for equal rights for men and women, aggressively advo-cating for women to have a vote. He was also ahead of his time in predicting that Canada would be a bilingual country, encour-aging his own children to be fluent in both English and French. Plus he created the Labour Day weekend (thank you, Sir John!).

Canada's reluctant leader

"I'm glad that I found him"

Sir John A. Macdonald was proud that he'd convinced John to join the Conservative party. Old John A. knew a good man when he saw one. And John was one of the best. A hard-working, capable man who hated injustice and cruelty, especially cruelty to women and children.

But John was a reluctant candidate for public life and an even more reluctant prime minister. He allowed himself to be pushed into several career moves he didn't want to make. For instance, he already had a successful career as a lawyer when his wife cajoled him into becoming a politician. And once he'd settled in as a provincial politician, he let himself be arm-twisted into becoming the attorney general of Canada, requiring that he move away from Nova Scotia, to Ottawa. Something similar happened again when 72-year-old Sir John Abbott became Canada's third prime minister. Everyone knew it was really John who was running the government. When Abbott resigned the following year, John was persuaded to accept the post of prime minister.

PM, interrupted

Although he spent almost half of his life in politics and worked hard at doing what he did, he fell short of making the full contribution he certainly had the potential to make. And because of that, few Canadians today have even heard of him. He has become Canada's forgotten prime minister.

47

Glossary: words and facts you might want to know

Aberdeen, Lady (1857–1939): born Ishbel Maria Marjoribanks, she was the wife of Lord Aberdeen, who was governor general of Canada from 1893 to 1898. She was active in the struggle to increase women's rights in society.

Aberdeen, Lord (1847–1934): seventh governor general of Canada (1893–1898). Born John Campbell Hamilton Gordon in Edinburgh, Scotland, he moved to Canada for the time that he was governor general.

Abbott, Sir John Joseph Caldwell (1821–1893): Canada's third prime minister (1891–1892) and first prime minister born in Canada, at St-André-Est, Lower Canada. When Sir John A. Macdonald died in 1891, Sir John Abbott was selected to take over, the first prime minister to serve from the Senate. Due to ill health, he turned over the government to Sir John Thompson in 1892.

Affleck, Annie (1845–1913): born in Halifax, Annie was the wife of Sir John Sparrow David Thompson. She and John married in 1870. She gave birth to nine children, five of whom survived to adulthood.

alderman: an elected member of a city council who helps decide how the city will run. The city council is made up of aldermen and the mayor. During council meetings, aldermen discuss and vote on issues like fixing the streets, maintaining the public libraries, and recycling garbage. In some cities, this position is called "councillor."

attorney general: in federal and provincial governments, an elected member of the legislature and a member of cabinet. The attorney general is the chief law officer and is responsible for the proper administration of justice in the country or province. In the federal government, the minister of justice is also the attorney general of Canada. Duties include representing the government in civil and criminal cases.

bar: official association of people who practise law. It is responsible for the regulation of the legal profession in its region. After studying law in university then articling in a law firm—or, as in Sir John's time, apprenticing with another lawyer or lawyers—students write the bar examination. They are then "called to the bar," which means they can start practising law as a profession.

Bell, John Allison (1816–1901): family friend of Sir John Thompson and Halifax city auditor from 1875 to 1901.

Bering Sea Tribunal: a special international court of justice set up in 1893 to judge whether the United States had the right to deny seal hunting by Canadians in open waters near the Pribilof Islands of Alaska. From 1886 to 1890, seventeen Canadian sealing ships were seized by the United States. Eight judges from Great Britain, United States, France, Italy, Sweden, and Norway were appointed to listen to the case. Canadians were found to have had the right to hunt seals in international waters, but the tribunal imposed restrictions for future hunting. The United States was later ordered to pay almost $500,000 in damages to Canada.

Black Empire Loyalists: Black people who left the newly formed United States between 1783 and 1785 after Great Britain lost its colonies in the American Revolution (1775–1783). Black slaves and servants who fought for the British were offered freedom and land for their services. Some 5,000 black people left for Nova Scotia, the West Indies, Quebec, England, Germany, and Belgium. Their names were recorded in a document called the *Book of Negroes*.

Blake, Edward (1833–1912): Liberal party politician in both the Ontario and federal governments. He succeeded Alexander Mackenzie as Liberal party leader in 1880 but lost the elections of 1882 and 1887. He then resigned his leadership and eventually left Canadian politics in 1891. This made him the only leader of the Liberal Party of Canada not to become prime minister.

board of trade: an association of business owners who join together to protect and promote business interests in their area. Members can network with each other and receive and provide support. The board also communicates the business concerns of its members to governments.

Bowell, Sir Mackenzie (1823–1917): fifth prime minister of Canada (1894–1896). Born in England, he arrived in Canada in 1832. He was appointed prime minister after the death of Sir John Thompson. Following an election loss in 1896, he led the Opposition from the Senate until 1906.

More words and facts you might want to know

Bright's disease: an old term that was used for any type of kidney disease or disorder. It was used by doctors as late as 1913.

British Empire: an old term that refers to Great Britain, all of its dependent countries and provinces, and the British dominions in the world.

cabinet: a group of members of the legislature (House of Commons or the Senate) who have been invited by the prime minister to head a major government department or ministry of state.

Cameron, Right Reverend John (Bishop of Antigonish): friend of Sir John Thompson and Roman Catholic bishop in Nova Scotia. His support of John was well-known and John sought his advice on many political matters.

Confederation: the union of states or provinces to form a new country.

congress: the legislature of the United States government. This is where the laws are made.

Conservative Party of Canada: the first party to govern Canada. It was formed in 1854 when politicians from Upper and Lower Canada united to form the government of the Province of Canada. In the beginning it was called the Liberal-Conservative party but later changed its name to Conservative when a separate Liberal party was formed at the time of Confederation. Sir John A. Macdonald was its first leader.

criminal code: collection of government laws that describe what a country considers to be criminal offences. It also provides the maximum and minimum punishments that courts can impose on offenders when such crimes are committed.

Dalhousie Law School: founded in 1883, it is the oldest university-affiliated common law school in the British Commonwealth and the first university law program outside of Quebec. Sir John Thompson was instrumental in founding the school because he believed that learning to be a lawyer through apprenticeship provided inadequate training.

First Nations peoples: the descendants of the first inhabitants of North America. The constitution recognizes three groups of aboriginal people: Indians, Métis, and Inuit. These are three separate groups of people with unique heritages, languages, cultural practices, and spiritual beliefs.

governor general: the representative of the British Queen or King in Canada who provides the royal assent necessary for all laws passed by Parliament. The governor general is a figurehead who performs only symbolic, formal, ceremonial, and cultural duties, and whose job is to encourage Canadian excellence, identity, unity, and leadership. Governors general are Canadian citizens appointed for terms of approximately five years.

High Commission: the place where an independent Commonwealth country, like Canada, is represented in the capital city of another independent Commonwealth country. The most senior representative is called the high commissioner. In London, England, Canada House is Canada's High Commission. In other countries, Canada maintains embassies and the senior representatives are called ambassadors.

House of Commons: the lower house of Parliament. It consists of a speaker, the prime minister and his cabinet, members of the governing party, members of the opposition parties, and sometimes a few independents (elected members who do not belong to an official party). The members of the House (commonly called members of Parliament or MPs) are elected by the Canadian people and currently number 308. The House (often incorrectly referred to as Parliament) is important because all new laws in Canada begin here.

Howe, Joseph (1804–1873): premier of Nova Scotia (1860–1863). Born in Halifax, Joseph was a controversial journalist before entering politics. He led the opposition forces against Confederation.

Jesuit Estates Act: passed in July 1888 by the Quebec Legislative Assembly, this act required the Quebec government to pay $460,000 to the Jesuits, Laval University, and several Roman Catholic dioceses. Various Protestant institutions received part of this payment as well. The Jesuits had originally launched a campaign to receive compensation for the land that the British took following the Seven Years' War. Many people in Ontario disagreed with this act and tried to have the federal government reverse it.

More words and facts you might want to know

knighthood: to be honoured with the title of "Sir" by a king or queen as a reward for personal excellence or services provided to the crown or country.

Labour Day: a holiday at the end of summer, created to celebrate workers and their families.

Liberal Party of Canada: one of the major political parties in Canada. It traces its history back to the Reform party in the Province of Canada in the mid-19th century. The Reformers led the opposition to the ruling Conservatives and campaigned for responsible government (more control for the elected members of the government). They didn't form an organized party until the time of Confederation (1867), when they called themselves the Liberal party.

Macdonald, Sir John A. (1815–1891): Canada's first prime minister (1867–1873, 1878–1891). He spent many years working to bring the Province of Canada and the Maritime provinces together. On July 1, 1867, his dream came true with the creation of the Dominion of Canada.

member of Parliament (MP): politician who is elected to sit in the House of Commons. During a general election, the country is divided into ridings (or constituencies). The voters in each riding elect one candidate to represent them as their MP in the government.

Métis: a person whose ancestry is half First Nations and half European origin (namely French and Scottish). Métis culture combines both backgrounds.

Methodist: Protestant religion that has roots in the Anglican church of England in the 18th century. It spread to the Maritime provinces of British North America in the latter part of the century. It was tradition to go out and preach to find new believers.

Mi'kmaq: the first peoples of what is now known as Nova Scotia, Prince Edward Island, the Gaspé peninsula, the islands in the Gulf of St. Lawrence and parts of New Brunswick, Newfoundland, and Maine in the United States. They call themselves *L'nu'k*, which means "the people." The term *Mi'kmaq* comes from a word that means "my friends."

Mercier, Honoré (1840–1894): premier of Quebec (1887–1891). He became leader of a French-Canadian party, Parti National, which he had helped to create.

Mowat, Sir Oliver (1820–1903): premier of Ontario for 24 years (1872–1896). He entered politics in 1858 as a member of the Province of Canada's assembly. As premier of Ontario, he was rewarded for his good direction by winning election after election. He raised many legal challenges to the federal government's powers, which resulted in the federal government recognizing that there were limits to its powers. In 1896, he retired as premier to become justice minister in Sir Wilfrid Laurier's government. He became a senator and lieutenant governor of Ontario.

National Council of Women: founded in 1893 at a public meeting in Toronto, chaired by Lady Aberdeen, wife of the governor general of Canada, and attended by 1,500 women. Its goal is to improve conditions of life for women, families, and communities by public education and meeting with politicians.

North West Mounted Police (NWMP): formed in 1873 by the government of Canada to keep law and order in the Northwest Territories. In 1919, the name of the police force was changed to the Royal Canadian Mounted Police (RCMP), which still exists today as Canada's federal police force.

Nova Scotia Supreme Court: established in 1754, it is the highest trial court in the province. From 1841, it had the power to make judgments over most criminal and civil cases, leaving minor offences and civil matters in the hands of local justices of the peace.

Parliament Hill: in Ottawa, Ontario, the complex of federal government buildings made up of the Centre Block, East and West Blocks, and the Library of Parliament. The House of Commons, Senate, MPs' offices, and committee rooms are located here.

parliamentary session: period of time that government representatives in the House of Commons and the Senate meet and execute government business. The session begins with the governor general's Speech from the Throne and lasts until "prorogation," when most meetings stop but Parliament does not dissolve. "Parliamentary session" is sometimes mistakenly associated with the Christmas and summer recesses of Parliament. Committees often meet during

Still more words and facts you might want to know

these recesses, which is normal because the session is still in progress.

Pier 21: a Halifax, Nova Scotia, gateway into Canada that was used from 1928 to 1971. During these years more than one million people entered Canada here and almost half a million Canadian service personnel left to serve overseas during World War II.

Privy Council: group of people who acted as advisers to the Crown. Sir John S. D. Thompson was sworn into the Council on the day he died. He was only the second Canadian to be so honoured, the first one being Sir John A. Macdonald.

public money: all money received and distributed by a public body, like a government. Also included is all money that is raised by a private body for a public body. Governments use this money to provide services for their citizens and foreign countries.

Queen Victoria (1819–1901): Queen of the United Kingdom of Great Britain and Ireland (1837–1901) and empress of India (1876–1901). During her reign, the English monarchy took on its modern ceremonial (non-ruling) character.

Riel, Louis (1844–1885): a Métis lawyer who led two armed rebellions against the Canadian government to defend the rights and lands of the French and First Nations peoples in the territories that later became Manitoba and Saskatchewan.

Roman Catholicism: the largest of the four branches of Christianity, the others being the Anglican Communion, various Protestant denominations, and Eastern Orthodox churches. During the fourth century, it became the official religion of the Roman Empire. The power of the Bishop of Rome, the Pope, gradually increased as Christian missionaries converted people throughout western and northern Europe. It spread to the Americas in the late 1400s. The Protestant Reformation in the 1500s ended the church's religious monopoly in western Europe. It still remains the largest single Christian religion.

Scott, Thomas: an Irish immigrant who was executed on the orders of Louis Riel on March 4, 1870. He opposed Riel's provisional government of the Red River settlement (now Winnipeg) and was ultimately convicted of insubordination while a prisoner. His punishment: death by firing squad.

Seven Years' War (1756–1763): first war that involved many nations. Britain, Prussia, and Hanover (now parts of Germany) fought against France, Austria, Sweden, Saxony (now part of Germany), Russia, and Spain. Britain tried to eliminate France as a commercial competitor. France lost all of its North American land except for St. Pierre and Miquelon in the St. Lawrence River and Martinique and Guadeloupe in the Caribbean.

Supreme Court of Canada: the highest court for all legal issues since 1949. The court is made up of a chief justice (judge) and eight junior judges. It advises the federal and provincial governments about interpreting the constitution. It is also a court of appeal for criminal and civil cases.

Treaty of Washington: signed in 1871 and in effect from 1873, an agreement between Great Britain and the United States that gave American fishermen access to Canadian fishing grounds for 12 years in exchange for $5,500,000. Canadian companies were given permission to sell their fish in the US market.

Tupper, Sir Charles (1821–1915): sixth prime minister of Canada from May 1 to July 8, 1896—69 days. He was one of the Fathers of Confederation.

United Empire Loyalists: people who remained loyal to the British Empire during the American Revolution (1775–1783). At the end of the revolution, they left the newly formed United States rather than become citizens. Thousands of them settled in Canada.

United States senate: the upper house of the United States congress, where elected members, or senators, propose and vote on legislation (laws).

visitors' galleries: also known as the public galleries of the Senate and the House of Commons. When the Senate or the House of Commons is sitting, visitors may watch the proceedings from the galleries.

Windsor Castle: one of the main official residences of the British monarch. The others are Buckingham Palace in London, England, and the Palace of Holyroodhouse in Edinburgh, Scotland. The castle is located in the town of Windsor, west of London. It is used for both state and private entertaining.

For more information on the terms listed in this glossary, visit www.jackfruitpress.com

Timeline: The life and times of Sir John S. D. Thompson

YEAR	JOHN'S LIFE	EVENTS IN CANADA AND THE WORLD
1844	John David Thompson is born on November 10 in Halifax, Nova Scotia.	Construction of the first railway in New Brunswick begins.
1847	John's sister Jane dies, age 15.	The St. Lawrence Canal is completed.
1848	John's sister Mary dies, age 18.	
1850		The Fugitive Slave Act is passed in the United States. This results in more free and enslaved black people fleeing to British North America.
1851		The first Canadian postage stamp is issued.
1852		In Chatham, Canada West, Mary Ann Shadd Cary becomes the first woman in North America to hold the position of newspaper editor.
1853	John's brother, William, is appointed deputy surveyor in Lunenburg County.	
1857		Ottawa becomes the capital of the Province of Canada. The revolt of 1857 takes place when India fights for freedom from British rule.
1859	John's brother, William, is dismissed from his job.	Abraham Shadd becomes the first black person elected to public office in Canada.
1860	John's father sells the family home to pay back money that William owes. John begins to use his father's middle name, Sparrow, in his own name. He starts work in the law office of Nepean Clarke.	Construction begins on the House of Commons.
1861	John begins articling with the lawyer Henry Pryor.	The US Civil War (1861–1865) begins: President Abraham Lincoln and the northern states want to abolish slavery. The southern states form a provisional "Confederate" government and go to war against the North. The North wins and slavery is ended.
1865	John writes the bar examinations and is admitted to the bar of Nova Scotia.	Slavery is abolished in the United States. The Salvation Army is founded in London, England, to serve the poor and homeless.
1867	John supplements his law income by reporting debates in the Nova Scotia Assembly as an assistant to J. G. Bourinot. His father, John Sparrow, dies. John begins to date Annie Affleck.	Canadian Confederation takes effect on July 1. John A. Macdonald becomes the first prime minister of Canada (1867–1873).
1868	John becomes lead reporter for the Nova Scotia Assembly.	The Federal Militia Act creates the first Canadian army.
1869	John becomes a law partner of Joseph Coombes.	Métis leader Louis Riel seizes Fort Garry, Winnipeg, during the Red River Rebellion to protest against the Canadian government not consulting with the Métis people before the Hudson's Bay Company handed over its land to the Canadian government.

More on the life and times of Sir John S. D. Thompson

YEAR	JOHN'S LIFE	EVENTS IN CANADA AND THE WORLD
1870	John and Annie are married in Portland, Maine.	Thomas Scott is executed under Louis Riel's provisional government. The Northwest Territories and the province of Manitoba are created.
1871	John converts to the Roman Catholic faith. John and Annie's first baby dies half an hour after being born. John is elected alderman of the city council of Halifax.	British Columbia joins Confederation. The Washington Treaty is signed between Great Britain and the United States to end fishing disputes in Canadian waters. The Franco-Prussian War ends (1870–1871).
1872	John buys his first house, called Willow Park. Their second baby, John Thomas Connolly, is born.	The first nationwide labour protest is held. Asian and aboriginal peoples are banned from voting in British Columbia.
1873	John gives up reporting debates in the Nova Scotia Assembly.	Sir John A. Macdonald is forced to resign as prime minister because of the Pacific Scandal. Prince Edward Island joins the Dominion of Canada. Alexander Mackenzie becomes the second prime minister of Canada (1873–1878). The North West Mounted Police force is formed.
1874	John's second son, Joseph, is born.	Iceland becomes independent of Denmark.
1875		The Supreme Court of Canada is established. The Indian Act is passed.
1876	His first daughter, Mary Aloysia ("Babe"), is born in March.	Alexander Graham Bell invents the telephone.
1877	John is hired by the United States to defend its fishing rights in Canadian waters. John runs for and wins his first seat in the Nova Scotia Legislature.	
1878	His second daughter, Mary Helena, is born in March.	Sir John A. Macdonald is elected for a second term as prime minister (1878–1891). The Canada Temperance Act is passed.
1880	John's son is born dead or dies the same day.	Edward Hanlan, a rower, becomes Canada's first world sports champion. Emily Stowe becomes the first female doctor to practise in Canada.
1881	John's third daughter, Frances Alice ("Frankie"), is born in December.	
1882	John is appointed leader of the Nova Scotia Conservative party and premier of the province. He resigns as leader and premier to become a judge on the Supreme Court of Nova Scotia.	The United States bans Chinese immigrants for 10 years. The world's first hydroelectric power plant begins operation on the Fox River in Appleton, Wisconsin.

Still more on the life and times of Sir John S. D. Thompson

YEAR		JOHN'S LIFE	EVENTS IN CANADA AND THE WORLD
1883		John is one of the founders of the Dalhousie University law school. He lectures on evidence. A son, David Anthony, is born.	The Sino-French War (1883–1885) starts: France and China fight over Vietnam. In the end, Vietnam is divided. China controls the north, France gets the south.
1885		John becomes minister of justice in Sir John A. Macdonald's federal government. His son, David Anthony, dies.	The Canadian Pacific Railway is completed. Canada's first national park is created in Banff, Alberta. The Northwest Rebellion takes place. Louis Riel is hanged for treason. The federal government imposes a head tax of $50 on Chinese immigrants.
1887		John is re-elected in the federal election. His mother, Charlotte Pottinger Thompson, dies. John is appointed legal adviser to Charles Tupper during negotiations in Washington to end the fishing dispute with the United States.	The first colonial conference takes place in London. Queen Victoria celebrates her golden (50-year) jubilee.
1888		John is knighted for his work on resolving the fishing dispute. John's family moves to Ottawa.	The Fisheries Treaty is passed. The first election takes place in the Northwest Territories.
1890			The Manitoba School Act is passed.
1891		John introduces a codification of Canada's criminal laws into Parliament for debate.	Sir John A. Macdonald dies while in office. John Abbott becomes the third prime minister of Canada (1891–1892).
1892		John becomes the fourth prime minister of Canada.	The Canadian Criminal Code is established.
1893		John is appointed a judge on the Bering Sea Tribunal that takes place in Paris, France. He's called to the Imperial Privy Council.	The Bering Sea Tribunal decides that Canadians have the right to hunt seals in the Bering Sea.
1894		John travels to Great Britain to be invested into the Imperial Privy Council. He dies soon after at Windsor Castle.	Sir Mackenzie Bowell becomes the fifth prime minister of Canada (1894–1896).
1895		John's body arrives back in Canada. His funeral is held in Halifax, after which he is buried in Holy Cross Cemetery.	Guglielmo Marconi invents the wireless telegraph in Italy.

Index

Is this a great country or what?

We've got the Rockies, the Mounties,
the Prairies, and the Barenaked Ladies.

And how about those Prime Ministers?
In their own way, they're a natural wonder too.
Each one as different as a snowflake...

Some of them made us laugh,
some made us cringe.
Others even made us furious.

Get to know each one.
One at a time.
Warts and all.